POETRY
OF SONG
TANGO
& JAZZ

POETRY
OF SONG
TANGO
& JAZZ

Poems by Richard Roe

Copyright © 2019 Estate of Richard Roe
All rights reserved

ISBN 978-1-878660-00-8 (paperback)

Cover photo by Jenny Mealing:
commons.wikimedia.org/wiki/File:Tango-Show-Buenos-Aires-01.jpg
Interior illustrations by Meghan Schultz
Book design by F. J. Bergmann, fibitz.com

First Printing

Fireweed Press
fireweedpoetry.com

To my wife, Barb,
and daughters, Meghan and Meredith

For the Madison Tango Society:
Tony DeGregoria
Jen Sutherland
Doug Reuhl

Table of Contents

Part One: Song

Song Full of Flowers	3
A Life in Music	4
The Forty-Oners	6
Folk Singer	8
The Lesson	9
Dental Serenade	10
Attempting to Sing "Something to Live For": the Billy Strayhorn Experience	12
Lines for the Most Miserable Country Song Anyone Will Ever Sing	13
The Burning	14
I Heard She Died	16
Excuses for the Blues	17
Two Conversations and a Song	18
The Powers of Singing	20
Dancing	21

Part Two: Tango

Autumn Whispers	25
Dance Lessons	26
Tango Lessons	28
On Intentions	29
A Tale of One Urban Night	30
May I Have This Reasonably Doubtful Tango	33
Tango Class # 333	34
Juega (Play)	36
Snow Dance	37
Late-Night Thoughts on the Tango: A Three-Dance Tanda	38

I Want to Tango with My Barber (Who Gives Me Head Massages)	41
The Day After	42
Tango Dreams	44

Part Three: Jazz

Autumn Scenes for Jazz Combo	49
Autumn Piece for Jazz Combo	50
Jazz at Night, Union Terrace, Madison	51
The '41 Limited	52
Yes, She's a Jazz Singer	53
Miss Peggy Lee	54
This Spring I Will Dream of Mary Lou Williams on Jazz Piano	55
Toward Evening	56
That Mood Indigo	57
Olympians	60
Listening to Lester Young and Billie Holiday	61
Behind the Beat	62
Shepherd's Return	64

Song Full of Flowers

You're my thrill—an acrostic

Yarrow, my little feather, make me your sweet pepper.
Orange jewelweed, I'm impatient, burst your pods, open my
Umbrella like mayapple leaves. I want hidden flowers, mandrake
's root. I dance rain's dotted rhythm, chase after your
Rough blazing star, long feather. Flaunt your flamenco dancer's
    skirt.
Evening primrose, we can sip wine at four, smell bouquets of

Mint leaves, bergamot tea. Lip balm, I'll be your long tongue.
Yucca, flower me upside down; spoon leaf, I'm Adam, bee
    hovering.

Trillium, curl your white petals; I'm an ant to your sticky seed.
Hyacinth, my blood spills for you. You are my accent in grape.
Rudbeckia, your dark eyes take me; cliché gypsy, I'm a yellow-
    petal capture.
Indigo, baptisia, dye me flower-white, your black pods disperse me.
Lupine, fix me, I'm your soil, your endangered butterfly, your
    blue July.
Larkspur, jingle me four-beat, tango at last. Blue shirt, whose is
    the next dance?

A Life in Music

My mother's family made their music on banjo,
fiddle, and guitar, and sometimes upright piano.
She grew up near those hills that seem to roll
all over each other, the only Amsterdam we know.

Rooster dawns, hound-dog evenings, and coal
smoke, the schoolhouse a five-mile walk away
in any weather, and the mine's tipple just below
the next ridge, my grandmother's household

knew that heaven inhabits a place in those hills
a beeline from the Methodist church's steeple.
Rock of ages, cleft for me, let me hide myself in thee.
If God didn't keep an eye out, your neighbors would.

My parents met singing hymns that climbed Jacob's
ladder, songs of love sweeter than sweet roses,
laments about death on a railway, and whatever
made it from Tin Pan Alley to eastern Ohio radio.

Life is like a mountain railroad, my mother sang,
with an engineer so brave, and the hills could hear her,
as my father chimed in in mountain tenor harmony
that could have made Ralph Stanley stand up and holler.

In my father's college days, oratorio, art song,
and opera fell on my parents like shining dawn.
Leise flehen meine Lieder durch die Nacht zu dir,
my father's Schubert crooned to my mother

as education served its veal cutlet, cordon bleu,
and cheesecake music with aged wine in tuned
goblets to raw country kids raised on hominy,
hindquarters stew, and succotash. A teacher

offered to train my father for an opera career,
but he gave up singing to declaim the qualities
for sinners to become standup Presbyterians.
Yet, Saturday was our Metropolitan Opera day,

when tenors and sopranos took leave of their senses
and stabbed each other longingly and passionately.
There I found my first love, Rise Stevens, my very
own Carmen. *L'amour est un oiseau rebelle que nul*

ne peut apprivoiser, she sang, me imagining her tangolike
walk, every ruffle of her low-cut blouse, those
insolent bare shoulders, and, oh, her betrayals.
I gambled on your love, Rise, and got a losing hand.

Too young to take to the bottle, I took to the blues
when I found out Rise was married, surrendered
my weekly allowance and my soul to rock and roll,
where I started over with every passing song.

The Forty-Oners

The years I rode the E-train to Queens,
took a bus to St. Alban's Naval Hospital,
Dylan and Baez, Richie Havens, and Paul
Simon and his friend Art aimed their guitars
at power on Fourth and Bleeker, in the Village.
Justice climbed their lyrics like arpeggios.

Dressed in starched whites, I joined the Hospital
Corps, drained wounds, cleaned up vomit,
blood, and shit. Patients jabbed at the cracks
in our well-plastered walls, raised the blinds.
I inserted catheters, gave penicillin injections,
and doled out pain pills. We were Pearl Harbor
babies, loosely bound by history, but we never met.

At St. Alban's, ten-cent movies furnished
our American dreams. We drank ten-cent
beer at the EM Club, staggered to our racks,
bragged about our aching heads. We traveled
to Radio City, Yankee Stadium, the Peppermint
Lounge, Jones Beach, and the bars in Queens
or on Long Island that served big burgers.

I left the Corps, left blood, catheters and injections
to others, put on button-downs, rode Greyhounds
to college, history and lit, beer kegs and Greek
parties, and hootenannies where the best picked
their brain matter clean on banjo and guitar,
drummed time away on bongos and table tops.

I put on authentic ragged jeans and real
torn sleeves, went sockless, my sailor's
vocabulary in vogue, hitchhiked to sing our
government into exile, end the Vietnam War:
guitars ready, aim, fire, Joan and Bob, Paul
and Art, Richie and thousands of marchers more.
We were on a first-name basis, but never met.

We survived, the song collections tell us that;
the lounges, the stadiums, the Navy Hospital
torn down, the festivals on film, our memoirs;
how, I ask and their voices give more answers
than I can sort out. The war is a black wall
with too many names. I raise a glass to all
of you. We've never met and my jeans
                    don't fit anymore.

Folk Singer

Wearing ragged jeans, a sleeveless shirt,
she works her way through songs
that travel all over this country,
naming café stops, rivers crossed, mountain
camps, and I'm along for the ride.

She taps her toes, stomps her feet, wraps her lips
around a harmonica, thumbs a road-life
beat on her bass string. Each finger picks
its own note, tells its part of the story.

I'm the main character in her love ballads
and laments, the listener for her new lyrics,
the one who supplies a word, a flower name,
flashlight batteries, little jokes, sweet rolls,
and directions not found on a map.

I want to hold her when she retunes her guitar,
nibble on her neck, her wrists, her knees.
After dark, I'll roll into her sleeping bag,
get up before dawn, drive her to another gig.

In the next song she praises my gray hair,
some wise thing I might have said,
gives me a cane-bottom rocking chair,
a porch in the shade, and strums and taps
her way across the Mississippi.

She sings my favorite, about a place in Colorado
where she meets a dream, the man who knows
her rhythm line before she does, that inconstant
bass player she wants to call *sweet daddy.*

The Lesson

for Maggie

Imagine the tallest tree in a forest
and you looking past clouds and mountain peaks.
Grip like a hawk and breathe until you sense
the tree's roots, trunk's length, the sap
rising, and push off. Feel the top of your skull
pulled by a taut string into sky's depths,
you shushing the wind; laugh in short bursts.
Fall and rise, ride to the knife-sharp edge of a draft,
giving the ride voice, calling *you, you,* and *we*
to anyone who could listen.

Believe you have a third eye, a space
sound rushes to like water from a pump.
Call like a siren. Draw lip-crisped
air past your teeth, form your abdomen
like the roundest of hills. Release, push
your midriff at the hard wood of your backbone,
letting an egg rest on your tongue
like the hollow space of a nest.
This is your sound: you are ready
to begin your first song.

Dental Serenade

Two young women, one with a metal
pick, the other holding a water jet,
stand over me wearing medical masks.

Pick and rinse, flick and suction,
open and close, wash and swish,
while a speaker plays a ballad

sung by some Christine or Nora
and the two technicians sing back
to the radio about being alone,

desire, the need to touch and be
touched, humming a phrase,
riffing on a string of words.

Open wide, she sings, and flosses
between the crevasses of my lab-
produced molar and bridge,

while the other one hums and rinses,
washes and swishes, tells me when
to open and close in a minor key.

I lie here on my back,
more helpless than an infant
who can at least cry or holler.

Everyone, my friend Mary croons,
needs to be sung to, and at my age,
my mouth numbed and my glasses

out of reach, my hands gripping
the chair's arm rests,
I am only allowed to imagine

strolling with two masked women
into Café Montmarte, asking Kelly
to sing her two best numbers.

Dedicating one to each,
a song she will sing
back to me at my next visit.

Attempting to Sing "Something to Live For": the Billy Strayhorn Experience

Most songs start and end on the same pitch,
like leaving through the front door and returning
the same way. Measure off time, count
the number of stops, follow traffic signals,
you're there, have lunch, come home on the chorus.
Not this song—it slips out the side door,
the key falls into tall grass. Time's steady enough,
but detours take you out of the way, your favorite
sandwich shop is closed, the salad you order contains
strange ingredients, and the way home is tricky.
The lyrics have the usual sentiments about love
as longing for adventure, a happiness to complete
the writer's life, life lived as a search. Hidden turns
tell you you're lost, another crooked street, but the score
ends at the bottom. You omit the verse, someone said
it's beautiful, but there are *cul-de-sacs* few singers
will brave. And then, when you do get home, you still
have a lost key and have to jimmy the back door.

Lines for the Most Miserable Country Song Anyone Will Ever Sing

I never thought I'd wind up like the man
in an old Johnny Cash song, half-dead
by a railroad track. But I don't hear any
songs out here, out of gas, battery gone
dead, shirt torn I don't know how, some
bar maybe, across the Dakota border.
I busted a window a mile back, no
satisfaction there, nothing to steal, home
not a place I want to be. I can't look
at anyone's eyes, just their backs, necks,
shirt collars. I've lost all the sleep I'm
going to lose, luck has leaked my radiator
dry, can't write a simple rhyme scheme,
and tomorrow will never find me.

The Burning

> *Love is a burning thing*
> *And it makes a fiery ring*
> *Bound by wild desire*
> *I fell in to a ring of fire.*
> —June Carter & Merle Kilgore

Like a bottle of beer on a dare,
I chug down a mug of scalding
black coffee with four sugars
at a corner table in "The Pit,"
exam-cramming, paper-writing,
boozy weekend, busted romance.

Like a Slinky landing on a step,
Darlene sinks into a chair, laughs
like the wicked sister who steals
boyfriends; she's high-octane caffeine,
custard-filled doughnuts, a torch song,
a concert grand sharply tuned.

She says, *Bach and Glenn Gould*, I fugue
for the four voices of a torrid wind;
Errol Garner, leaves falling on keyboards;
Earl Hines, keys dancing in infirmaries.
I mention my ex, and Darlene shakes
her hair, bountiful and wind-thrown

like a set of bellows fanning flames,
like the hip-slinging vamp of the gypsy's dance.
I can hear my roommate muttering clichés
about fires and frying pans, squared circles.
I'll skip the pep rally, leap into a flaming ring
and sizzle like sirloin on open fire at a beach bash.

Regret grins like a cruel relative,
leaves its rain check, instructions
for fire extinguishers. Beguile me
and burn me, douse me and leave
me a smoking ruin, my heart peeled
like scorched skin. Send Johnny Cash
                              for the dregs.

I Heard She Died

                    Yesterday
Odetta died, and I've got the blues.
The blues came when I heard Odetta died.
I've heard her voice in leaf-rattling winds,
in rain rapping on my roof, in call-
and-answer birdsongs before the sun
lights dayfires. Now Odetta's gone.

The Queen has passed over the river.
Jordan River's wide, but she passed over.
What a morning, Lord, so gray,
the slow-falling snow, the crack
in my voice, and her voice striding
baritone to soprano, water low or high.

Like hands that grip a shovel, that voice.
Listen to the voice gripping that shovel.
Dig deep for the mother of all children
who do not know their own.
Dig deep for the mother for our times,
marching on, glory, dry your tears, now,
free at last.

Excuses for the Blues

Woke up this morning begins a common refrain
for a blues song, twelve bars long, more or less,
smelling of empty beer cans, bourbon bottle
on its side. My jaw aches, the beer is gone,
you left me alone, will repeat to a shriek
from the electric guitar, the crooked gait
from the bass player, the drummer's back-beat,
insistent as a headache, the hangover, the blasted
pain from a slipped disk, the swollen balky knee,
the leg muscle torn up, walking stick out of reach,
and it rained all night, but that's another song,
rainy night in Waunakee, add an accordion,
a mouth harp, big mama from Winnetka
hollering to a slow-motion polka. Her squeeze
is gone, took all of her money, her joy juice.
You're kidding, the critic whines, *It's so,* I say,
'cause the blues only needs the flimsiest excuse.

Two Conversations and a Song

One:
Did you see how his lips tremble,
how slowly he walks,
feel how cold his hands are?
He will come and sit at our table,
pretend nothing's wrong.

I think death speaks softly,
answers your questions politely
with a smile and a nod.
He smells like aftershave
from a barber shop.

Look who's dancing with him,
the woman wearing a navy-
blue jacket and plaid skirt.
She'll be the death of him,
kissing his cheek, rubbing his neck.

She smells like lavender soap,
will reveal nothing of her intent
until she embraces him
at the most impossible moment.

Two:
Heine said death is the cool night.
You can hear more at night,
radio stations from Canada,
a whippoorwill repeating his name,
what the neighbors argue about.

Death whispers like a close friend
who wants to tell you her dream
(in strict confidence, of course),
like someone you could always trust.

Heine mentions the nightingale
rooted in his dreams.
I don't recall having that dream,
but think he means
a woman singing. She lulls you,
tells you the most interesting stories.

Ask her a question and she touches
your shoulder, ruffles your hair,
hums a melody you remember
from childhood in perfect pitch.

Song:
Piano, solo voice across the room,
the audience settles back.
Some because they are captive,
others for the love of pure sound.

She sings about night, the hot
cacophony of days, weariness,
what we hear in dreams.

What are we waiting for?
Are we beyond dreams?

She repeats the last phrase,
softly now, tapering to silence.
If I stop breathing, I'll never
hear the piano arpeggiate
the last chord, as if that matters.

The Powers of Singing

The first time we heard her sing "Caro nome" in Verdi's *Rigoletto*, we fell in love forever. Her fame spread from local stages to national and international opera houses, her voice dominating the air waves. Millions demanded recordings of her favorite arias and complete operas. One blue planet could not contain her. Astronauts carried her music into space. When new atmospheres were established at orbiting stations and nearby planets, pioneers demanded the sound of her voice, "a voice created by God," said the critics. Millions built their lives around her, creating monuments in her name. Rumors spread of animal sacrifices at altars beneath brazen images of her face.

"Blasphemy," cried the preachers, and the Voice That No One Knows began to speak in tongues. Storms frequented the blue planet and power went out in space colonies. The blue planet reversed its poles, wobbled erratically in its orbit. Sunspots grew like metastasized malignancies. Yet her voice rang with Puccini's "O mio babbino caro," and Purcell's "When I am laid in earth." The Voice That Could Not Be Named hissed like a thousand geysers followed by a great suction. The entire planetary structure flew out of kilter. Blackness devoured the solar system and the One Who Cannot Be Known roared. A last planetoid escaped the dark hole and her voice orbited into the Clouds of Magellan, while the Voice of Him Without a Name is lost, swallowed in the sounds of galactic winds.

Dancing

for Kay

My sister's husband taps and steps
to a Motown beat, call and response,
girl group, *baby love,* forward and back,
side to side, his eyes bright as strobe
lights, his grin like an ecstatic child's,
rolling his shoulders, snapping his fingers,
tossing his head, he gasps and giggles.

Bill loved to dance, my sister says,
in those clubs we went to Friday nights.
His mind fading like the end of a hit
record, his vocabulary reduced to *yeah,
you, who,* he finds grammar in motion,
the need to catch the beat, a language
                he can still understand.

The song dies away like Bill's memories,
but he wants to dance. We look
for a play box, buttons to select
a funky favorite, rhythm section
from Muscle Shoals, the horn chorus,
a night song, the river, coming home.
Bill blurts out a *yeah, another song,*
my sister says, *while there's time.*

PART TWO:

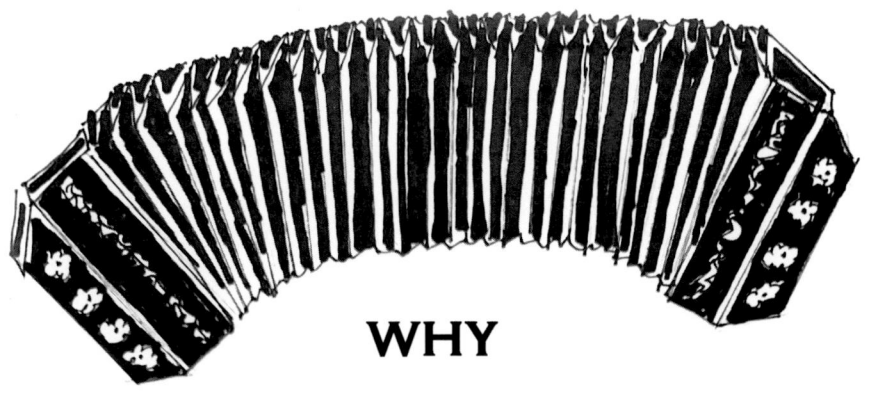

WHY

POETRY

LOVES

TANGO

Autumn Whispers

Tomorrow, I whisper, let's drive to Kettle Moraine,
Horicon, Door County, sugar maple red, quaking
aspen yellow, paper birch blonde, but tonight
your white swirly skirt, your high-heeled bright
red dancing shoes, your earrings in green and gold,
the soughing breath of a love song, a slow
breeze, trees in their coats of color, susurrus,
susurrus on a violin, step and slide, a tread
of soft landings, tango-red maples and scarlet
oak leaves, tamaracks in smoky yellow, the glow
when you lean against me, rocker steps, easy tempos
in twos and fours, the last set and the last dance
in sight, carmines, crimsons, and oranges, a chance
of evergreens, time's gestures, susurrus, susurrus.

Dance Lessons

There were no dancers in my family,
so Mom sent me to Mrs. Wilson's
dancing school to learn what
my Bible-thumping grandfather
preached against as sin.

They tried to teach me the box step,
fox trot, the cha-cha and lindy hop,
but what I remember best are nights
spent trying to do the tango.

Slow step, slow step, cross quick-quick,
turn, and again, and turn quick and dip,
the basic steps of the dance of love,
the body rub of desire, that kiss of fire,
part of my 12-step program to become suave.

I was fourteen, four-eyed, and blond,
sporting a flattop, peach-fuzz face
flowered with Old Spice aftershave,
skinny as a church-ritual palm frond,

picturing someone sassy, red rose in dark
hair, coals of fire eyes, a long-stemmed girl
with lubricated hips, and I got Betsy,
who was big, blonde, and blue-eyed.

She stared, transfixed, into my eyes,
smoothing strands of honey-dipped hair,
flicking her eyelashes, fixing her lips.
Glasses, she said, make good mirrors.

The music pulsed, and we glided away
to the *bump, bump, bar-ump, bump*
of the tango, my feet bouncing
like a ground ball on a bumpy infield.

And how Betsy moaned and gasped
under the spell of my size-nine loafers,
and asked how much I weighed,
said I was quite the partner.

So here's to you, you sideliners
who hide when the band strikes
up, you foot-shufflers, arrhythmics,
you whose dance posture reminds others
of grackles waddling on summer lawns.

But dream on, you dirty old men,
like I dream the band plays the tango
and she's there, dark hair, red rose.
We join thigh to thigh, hip to hip
like vine tendrils or Saran Wrap.

The dance that began in Argentine brothels
is recreated in ads for pants, computers
or overnight express, or in movies as steps
in idle and misspent lives that might
end in tragic or violent deaths.

I'm telling you this like it's a confession,
that Grandfather was right, it is about sin
and something wild never captured,
the elusive bird of passion, the dancer,
the dance, and even my boyhood grin.

Tango Lessons

I promised myself tango lessons
once the surgeon fixed my left hip.
Now, one evening a week, I learn
a dance as simple as walking.
My teacher tells me to lag behind
the beat like a jazz singer,
step lightly, don't march or bounce.
Tango is a conversation; partners
should hold hands so gently they can't
crumple a corsage. My conversation
already suffers when my teacher
adds hesitation, side steps, a way
to change weight, to vary my program.
Tonight, I learn the pivot where
my feet slant sideways, my upper
body still faces my partner.
Ah, the conversation tangles, jumbles,
but this is tango, where beginners, too,
can lament, weep, and start over.

On Intentions

Stand on your left leg, swing the right one, gently,
we do not kick here. Stand on your right leg,
bend the left, your heel touching your butt. Switch.
Lean forward at a slight angle, but keep your body
in line like a tower in wind. Shift weight from foot
to foot, decide on one, set, dip slightly from the knees.
That's intention, and here, intention is always good.
Repeat, partner's foot must start to slide but not step.
Repeat and step forward on the beat, do not stop,
as certainty must follow intention like walk lights
at a busy intersection. Speed is not important,
but dance must have continuity. Keep one foot
free of weight, the one that will move, using the balls
of your feet much like paws. When walking backward
make sure the toes land first, keep that forward lean,
posture like a palace guard, head up, alert to intentions
of others, the floor plans of tango dancers.

A Tale of One Urban Night

A woman dressed in a dark top
and pants quicksteps across
the floor of an abandoned warehouse.
Her head jerks like a nervous
bird on the lookout for predators.

A man steps out from the right.
His right arm flashes like a street
fighter pulling a blade; he motions
to the woman with his left hand.

When she goes to him, he grabs
her around her shoulders, walks
her in lock-step toward the back wall,
and stops, she twists away from him.

A second man appears in front of her
holding his arms out like a rescuer.
She bumps against him, puts her arms
around his neck. As they step away
the knife-fighter drops his hands.

The rescuer turns the woman in circles.
They lock in an embrace, constantly moving,
like a couple trying to escape a barroom
brawl through the back door.

A third man appears from the left.
He crouches, knees bent, hands
at ready like a boxer setting
up for a knockout punch.
He takes the woman by an arm.

She looks at him like a combatant,
stamps her right foot, tap-steps
her way around his feet,
stamps her left foot, he grabs
her hands, pulls her to his chest.

The other two men close in
like street thugs looking
for action. The boxer delivers
the woman into the arms
of the knife-fighter, she kicks

each of his legs, backs away,
leaps into the arms of the rescuer
who holds her for the moment,
then rejects her, pushing her
into the path of the boxer.

They have her surrounded.
I see an urban horror story
unfolding, assault, knife fight,
the woman dead, one or more
of the men down and bleeding.

I summon a rare burst
of courage, bang through a door,
holler *let her go*, on my way
to becoming an urban legend,

a headline in the morning paper,
a featured hero for *Reader's Digest*,
or an emergency-room statistic.
They glare at me like a brawling family
that has found a common enemy.

Do you tango? the woman asks.
Before I can answer, she takes
me into their circle like a backslider
into a prayer group that asks
for forgiveness, deliverance from sin.

Only now do I hear the bandoneon,
vibes, bass, guitar, and piano.
Can't dance at that tempo! I say,
but they grab hold and pull me along.

The woman laughs softly,
says they will show me the way
to walk, tame my wayward feet,
keep your knees bent, to let go,
a new chapter in dance magic,
an urban legend is born.

May I Have This Reasonably Doubtful Tango

So I put my weight on one foot,
the right (it helps to keep track),
the left foot itches, steps; don't
forget the rest of my body, in fact
the chest needs to stay in front.
Lean, not too much (I'm not stem or tower).
So she can cross, I step outside my partner—
but disassociate? Oh, walk one way
while my upper half quarter-twists another
and two, three steps ahead, collect my feet.
Keep the connection, I'm told, it belongs
in the realm of the sacred, my frame
a wobbly embrace, at half-mast her bad draw.
I'm the martyr-maker, derailer of tango dreams.
There are no arrivals in my moves, can't read
the schedule, my posture like an inside-out
umbrella, moves that mimic a partygoer
bobbing blindfolded and missing the apple;
road-kill potential, but too slow to try to cross.
I walk like someone who steps off a curb not
there; the sheep I count can't jump fences;
my kite loses its tail before it can fly.
Choreograph me as the duck that tried
to land and missed the pond, the heron that
speared its own foot, the mighty woodcock
spiraling and banging its head on a branch.
Yes, I'm the tricked coyote who's run out of cliff
and there's only air, elegance a match for a hedgehog.
I'm not the old shoe or worn sock, only the hole.

Tanģo Class #333

> *O chestnut tree, great rooted blossomer,*
> *Are you the leaf, the blossom or the bole?*
> *O body swayed to music, O brightening glance,*
> *How can we know the dancer from the dance?*
> —William Butler Yeats

OK, tonight we'll learn another way to get to a molinette
from a back ocho, and add more turns or ganchos.
I review turn, turn, turn. The instructor demonstrates
with an equally supple partner, *ochos*—their spot-on pivots
and floating back steps—*then, leaders step around*
your follow with your left foot, pause while she takes
a second step, and return to the line of dance.

A U-turn, I think, with a yield sign and merging traffic,
a kind of roundabout for walking—
But my pivot, it's canvas soles on fresh tar,
try again, and it's a wad of pink bubble gum
stuck to my left shoe. My right foot falls like a tree
with root rot. My partner must think she's hooked up
with Bigfoot, starts slip-stepping, tip-toeing.

Switch partners. Her *whoosh* tells the story.
My next victim dresses in her best smiles, the song
playing on iPod speaks to illusions and future
loneliness. My pivot skids and pops like a road
hauler with sticking brakes, navigator goes out of whack,
recalculating, I've gone the wrong way on the roundabout.

Switch partners, and now he says: *leaders keep your shoulders*
parallel to your followers. Eye contact tells me my partner wishes
I'd take up Texas two-step or square dancing.
I stretch obliques, dorsals, intercostals, that ripping sensation,
old cloth acting its age, hearing a song about how it burns,
a heart ripped apart, another flap-flap with my right foot,
brake chatter. My follower *ooohs* her sympathies.

This long-haul truck has a big turning radius. *Switch partners.*
I make a miraculous pivot, hold for one count, and we step
cleanly into the line of dance, the GPS bell dings, bows
find violin strings, partner nods her approval and we repeat
one time for the collection and the confessional.
Yes, says the instructor, *gather 'round, we're ready for some
really interesting moves,* stops, step-overs, more turns, exits
and entrances. You will know this truck by its driver.

Juega (Play)

Like a brush, her toe traces
his calf muscles. She hooks
her lower leg behind his thigh,
more than once is best,
steps, pivots, and walks
in front of him, a painter
studying her designs,
a few feet of floor space,
a canvas for dance notation.
He draws another line, line
flirts with toe, calf rubs calf,
a turn, a stroke of color,
two streams of paint
embrace.

Snow Dance

> *Oh friends, where can one find a partner*
> *for the long dance over the fields?*
> —William Stafford

The week her grandfather died, she recalled
dancing with him at her sister's wedding,
the gardenia, his neatly parted white hair,
a tango he likened to snow falling in calm wind.

You were quick to learn, he told her, and she
remembers his hand against her shoulder
blade, the front and back *ochos,* the circles
clockwise and counter, side-steps, crosses,

and step-overs, the kisses he gave her,
the stranger who commended him on finding
such a young and supple partner, his smile
when he said *she is my granddaughter.*

Standing here for reasons she refuses to talk about,
wanting to forget how much the world can hurt,
she thinks of him, catches snowflakes on her
sleeve, gardenias, some that join like couples

who dance together frequently, pines wet
with fresh snow. She walks across the field
alternating slow, quick, and slow steps,
holding her right palm up for a partner's left.

Crossing her left over her right ankle, she pivots,
brushing one leg against the other, stops
to catch a snowflake on her tongue, steps
through a point, begins a circle into all

the snowy afternoons she needs.

Late-Night Thoughts on the Tango: A Three-Dance Tanda

1.
Passion's a four-beat thump on bass,
a piano player's left hand.
Collect your feet as if they're thoughts
waiting to be written out.

Pretend you're on stage, signal the spotlight
to move with you, dialogue in four-foot lines
and walk into a story that begins
one night in the life of—pivot to expose

the secrets of hips that follow
chest and shoulder, reverse direction
because you're never lost—but a melody
repeating and embellishing its first statement.

A button accordion snarls and pleads,
the violin counters with its own complaints,
a guitar strums a get-along and move
to the next gesture, a betrayal of intent

that begs, "walk around me," revolving
like confessions of enjoyment, skirt swishes,
footwork's story: "watch me, catch me."
Walk that line as if the door's going to close.

2.

Oh, go ahead, step into each other's space,
your foot like a snake's tongue, the pivot's
narrow evasion, merry-go-round if you like,
blurry fairway lights, a chase scene on foot,

sidewalks and alleys, the mime's imaginary
staircase, the thrill from near collisions,
the pause that catches your breath,
satisfaction like a finger snap.

You are a singularity—an impeccable frame,
the hand-to-hand and arm-around of embrace,
the heart-to-heart of immaculate motion,
a complete turn on one foot, while you walk,

backward, slipping around someone you know,
shadow effect. Captivity's a moment, a movement,
it's a wrap leg to leg, it's a stop and wait, a leg hook,
set and released, consummated, repeated.

You want that look: slit-skirted leg
resting against black pants, dance heels
in silver, one foot in mid-air poised
for an easy landing, the burglar's touch.

3.
You are lost in transition,
the third dance, the set, the sidelines—
one move saved like a trump card,
a denouement, the moral of the story.

The pass is too swift, like a kick,
that false lead, a yelp like a cry of betrayal,
the empty space between two hearts.
A balloon deflates, a perfect icicle melts.

Nothing cries like the bandoneon's lament,
a chorus walked at arm's length, beginners'
class mechanics, the weeks of practice,
passion's sweat, its pinched toes, muscle cramps.

Lead to a back step and a stop, one foot
sandwiched between two, the move signaled,
toes rubbing the calf muscle, the step across
and you're in figure eights, poised on one foot.

Lean into a close embrace and walk lightly
left foot to left and right to right, crossing
to back turns that flow like the band's melodies
echoing the litany of tango's second chances.

I Want to Tango with My Barber (Who Gives Me Head Massages)

At last I'm next. My good
barber, Ideki, shakes her cloth,
coaxes me into her chair. *You have
designs on my hair.* Her laugh's as
electric as clippers prowling my neck.
Face dusted, she raises my chin,
grips great clumps of white
hair, cuts, *precise as tango,* I say. She
indulges me with a head massage, this
Japanese woman, she says, *make good dancer,
keep strict time, responsive,* and I
lure her to the aisle, clasp her in
my arms, hum an Argentine melody,
nudge her into motion. Leading
ochos forward and back, we
pivot across the shop, and
quick-step to a halt. She rises on her
right axis; I walk backward around her,
sleek as an Astaire disciple, marking a
turn to dance our way through a
universe of flying hair, scissors keeping time.
Vaulting into the air as I lift her, skirt fanning out,
warbling another tune, she crosses her ankles, a precise
x, changes weight, and hears
yira—turn, closes like a
zipper, its tab perfectly in place.

The Day After

Like a wine-and-drug hangover, this ache,
dry mouth, fat head, leg cramps, a slow
ear melody, but it's not last night's piece,
two as one in close embrace, a parade
of legs synchronized with the beat, tune
played by a live quartet, solid bass player,
the echo effect of every promenade and turn,
the flow like magic, miraculous as water.
More than any drug, Tango can possess you.

Today's music has an ache that owns you,
a duet of string work and bellows, time lapse
frames from post-midnight dancing, sadness
overtakes you—*el día después*—the day
after, your late-night partner not answering,
a slow fade, but the tune, this music will
never leave, replaying at odd moments
this Friday, next week, next month, a café,
swirly office, whirly sidewalks, stairwell.

A year, two years, excerpts from a dance
film, fragments from your favorite moves,
and that mournful music, the vocalese,
a woman's voice crying quiet desperation,
and when you cannot sleep, street noise
cymbals, sound effects are cold winds.
Legs no longer support your weight, acute
shortness of breath, blind in one eye, the moon
a sour lemon yellow, dance shoes given away.

In the end there's a swishing sound, tone
arm on an old turntable, an ending—you can
always play it again, until it's engraved in
your memory—even if fires and floods
destroy your collections, creating another
set of day-after memories, miraculous
as motion that flows in the synchronized
magic of a close embrace, two becoming one,
in tango's possession measure for measure.

Tango Dreams

for Doug Reuhl

The pianist plays a catch-breath rhythm
that can only mean the tango, a willing
partner who says count to eight
and don't look at your feet.
We stride, turn, and fan around
the floor like two cat burglars
dressed for action in panther black.

We are like the dancers at Renoir's café,
my right arm well around her, her hand
at the back of my neck, living the words
of libidinous conversations, punctuated
by *ah* and *my love*. The violin sings
a nostalgic melody over the hesitation
beat of the guitar and bandoneon.

The café doors open and dancers pour
into the street, mount mobile flatbeds
each with a four- or five-piece band.
Taken by surprise, we pause, turning our heads
every which way, like cameras panning
boulevards that stretch to an indefinite horizon.

We pass buildings reminiscent of other times,
balconies that have wrought-iron railings,
flower boxes spaced curbside at perfect
intervals, carts containing fresh fruit parked
at every corner, and milk and honey wagons
left on divider strips for our convenience.

We go by a quay lined with silver boats
rigged to sail among islands
that sprout a thousand varieties of lilies,
filled with talking birds, intelligent lemurs,
and ageless trees. The rigs carry names
like Blue Lagoon, Paradise Cove, Blue Bayou.

We are presented with keys to the Eternal City
where the state has withered away,
the invisible hand has turned into a vast
palm that offers conch shells,
gold rings, and green and red gems.
Here, it is said, the division of labor
and pleasure balances on infinite scales.

PART THREE:

JAZZ CORNERS

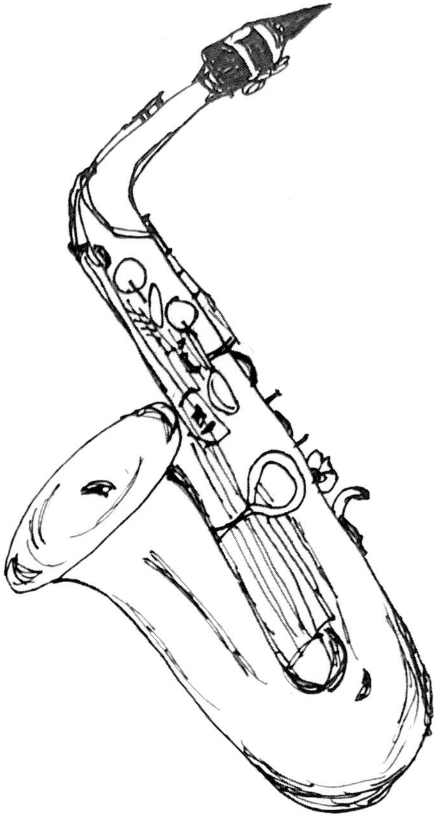

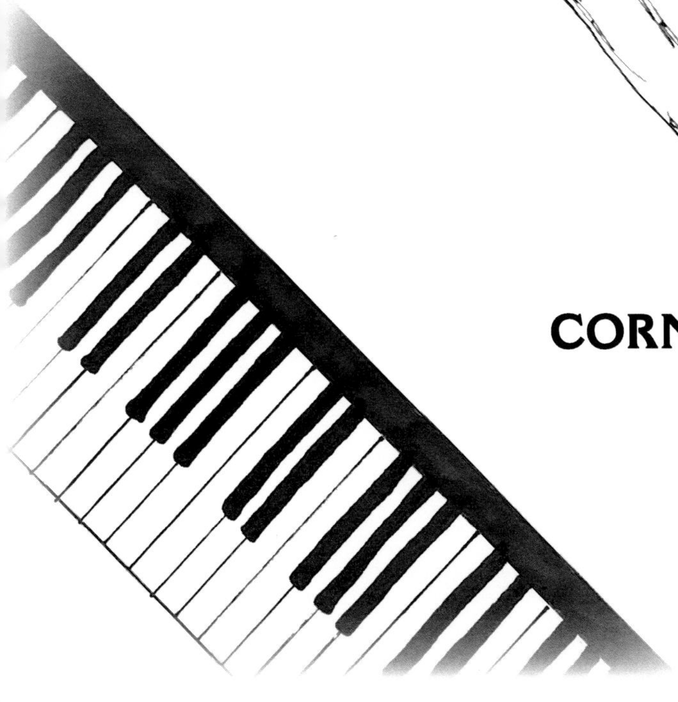

Autumn Scenes for Jazz Combo

1.

Footsteps on dirt, a trail,
a bass plucked, the drum
imitates nuts falling, repeats
the pattern, the sax honks
like geese on wing, some
leave, others stay, fade
in and out, cross a bridge,
piano part rises and falls,
finch looking for seeds.

2.

The piano plays a slow tempo,
chords like a hymn, the bass
every other beat, the drummer
a shuffle with brushes, an old
love letter, an arm-linked
couple, the sax plays a melody
that lingers like leaf colors
in memory, the trumpet
answers, pictures taken,
an evening walk.

Autumn Piece for Jazz Combo

That jagged song starts on a bass fiddle's
run, the voice of wind stripping trees.
Tenor sax and trumpet break in,
clash like a couple who quarrel
over yard work, while the piano
plays two-note chords that walk fast.
The drummer raps cymbals, snares,
blocks like the wind whacks at branches.
The muted trumpet moans cold rain,
a for-sale old place, moonlight haunts.
The sax picks up on short days passing,
the rhythm section rattles windows,
the trumpet plays chimney smoke.

Jazz at Night, Union Terrace, Madison

Hips swinging to two beats and three, two dancers
fast-step forward and back, break out, slide and tap
to the salsa band's beat. The conga player's hands
talk to each other, a trumpet blows on the sax's
twisting line; they circle like two people in want,
looping into a chorus like the dancers who pass
palms, turn under each other's arms, wrap around twice,
embracing belly to back under a June night's sky
when clouds stretch and split, spilling orange stripes
like paint along the edge of a world as immediate
as salsa jazz and two young dancers, their laughter
the breezes that sway boats and rattle anchor chains.
They stumble, as they must. The lights are turned out,
leaving only the moon and an old poet slipping anchor.

The '41 Limited

The year I rode into the world
Duke Ellington took the A-train
to Harlem, its clubs, its theaters,
and Coleman Hawkins and Ella came
speaking in jazz, fluent in blues.
It's the heart that needed fire, not the globe.
I arrived early, by as much as ten days,
yelling at lights I saw. Fires, out of control,
burned over horizons, smoke-filled raids
drummed all night, blues for bodies and souls.
Khaki brown and olive drab rode our trains.
They wrote the songs I'd sing in my old age.

Yes, She's a Jazz Singer

I tap my toes when Mary, on cello, plucks
the theme, a scotch-and-soda tune, her song
about an evening we can stroll and strut
away our aches, her dimples promising salt-laden
shoreline breezes; drummer brushes
his traps, touches cymbals and rattles; I stand
and join Mary in song, a ricochet chorus
of vowels, scatted nonsense, clapping my hands.

Guitar plays a siren's call, a night fire's burn;
cello and piano orbit, voice Venus-high.
Red moon catches clams and mussels, sauce and Saturn,
meteor's flash, coals glowing for night's reprise.
Sustained notes sit me down, tone-tied and wrapped
in chords and changes, a voice that says *you're back*.

Miss Peggy Lee

In hair-grease days when rockabilly songs
and doo-wop groups nearly ruined my brain,
I could hear Peggy Lee telling me
I give her fever, fervor, sweet kisses,
those *do-me-right* night sweats.
Oh, lover Peggy, buxom, platinum blonde,
that perfect mole on your right cheek,
hold me against your breasts,
croon like a breeze filling sails on Dream Lake,
shake your bare shoulders to keep me in time,
wink when you lag just behind the beat.

Tonight I will hear you sing
be anything, but darling be mine,
picture your scoop-necked, tight-fitting
white gown, spotlight catching its sequins.
Your hand resting on the piano could melt
its strings, your voice would turn my brain
to candle wax that drips from my ears,
down my cheeks, my jaw, and neck.
And when you ask *is that all there is?*
I say *yes,* but sizzle, baby, burn my sky.
From chills to fever to love in A-minor,
you, Peggy, thermostat, pilot light, and flame.

This Spring I Will Dream
of Mary Lou Williams on Jazz Piano

for Fabu

      when crocuses unfurl
in purple, the first leaves pop open
on maple, crabapple, and lilac—
will see someone's son, glasses
falling down his nose, fingering
one of Mary Lou's angular melodies
in his right hand, left-hand accents
she taught playing tag—
sandhill cranes boom in a marsh,
cardinals and grackles strut for mates.
Bekka's long fingers will spell gospel
chords that wind like stems climbing
my side-yard fence, brazen blue skies
in late May, my garden an obsession
in blues, delphinium, lobelia, bellflower—
morning glory with blooms like the blue
in candle flames, and she will ask me,
      again, *what's your story?*

Toward Evening

—Thelonious Monk, "Crepuscule with Nellie"

You take a bite of morning bun
and what I want to say is I— but never mind:
the phone, the door. You and your sisters
talk all morning under the canvas shelter
we bought. You said cut the grass,
pull the weeds, trim, re-stake the corners.
My words won't enter that shelter, where
your older sister naps in the afternoon,
your younger sister inside, her sons
a kitchen of trouble, two crème doughnuts
and a hazelnut coffee's worth, both
of our daughters talking, one here, one on cell phone,
all those grandsons, more trouble, lots of chocolate bars,
your coffee's cold, talk all day, half-empty cups
everywhere, and I'm too slow to say—too frazzled
to shout. Your brother and family pull in
from Wyoming; you're all together, first time
                      since your dad died.

Evening breather: you ask who's on the piano,
good melody line, like a slow exhale,
Monk, I say, for Nelly, his wife—
the piano's hesitation, a little dissonance
like a chuckle, rhythm section catches up.
I watch where your lips touch the cup,
the sip I want of your coffee.

That Mood Indigo

> 'Cause there's nobody who cares about me
> I'm just a soul who's bluer than blue can be
> When I get that mood indigo
> I could lay me down and die.
>   —Ellington, Mills & Bigard

1.

It's like sitting alone, watching television,
a movie that seems vaguely familiar—
someone's gone away, someone else looks
for that someone and there's no one to tell
you, you have already seen it more than once.

2.

Lately you've been morose.
People ask if you're O.K.
You used to like their little jokes,
the stories, but now it seems
they want to spill the crumbs
of their lives on your lap,
an endless trail of faithless lovers,
fights with the boss, impossible
children—they're cobwebs
in your face, burrs sticking
to your pants—you itch
to brush them off.

You want to play solitaire
but have no idea where
you put the deck of cards.
So there's no use and besides
you don't like the way the jacks
stare at the queen of hearts.

3.
Looking out the window at night,
the moon's an orange blaze;
its light stings like sleet.
Stars are the words on a page
you can't comprehend.
Jettison the moon, it shows
you dark circles under your eyes.
Cover the stars, put the book
away, don't bother to mark the page.

The radio plays a number you requested
at a small café, jazz trio, bass player's
yellow fingertips on blue strings—
used to sing it as a duet, making up
nonsense syllables, little love words.
You can't turn it off, this melody that blue
would sing if it could—haven't gotten
around to those "cure for blues"
clichés sent by friends.

4.

It's a song Ella sang at Duke's place,
that blue kind of rightness,
like a navy dress trimmed with white lace.
You sit alone sipping tea with honey,
nibbling on a hazy blue memory.

Ella—you heard her live years ago
in Jersey, phrases that sipped your tea,
pianist's chords squeezing lemon slices.
Let memory take its course,
the song repeat its chorus,
and wait for that last phrase,
hold on to that last note
as long as you can.

Olympians

Lester Young's tenor sax loops around
songlines from Billie Holiday's lips,
and today, a pair of ice skaters take
their act to a rink, executing double
toe loops, lifts, tosses, and flips.

The program they've arranged to music
could be their story, like a song's story
Billie tells as her own, *time on my hands
and you in my arms.* Lester matches
Billie's vibrato, her words lurking in his
mouthpiece, waiting for him to blow.

The skaters glissade to every corner
of the rink, blades cutting measures
in ice, spinning on point, and in *ooh
what a little moonlight can do,* Lester
swings Billie to her final note.

Listening to Lester Young and Billie Holiday

When Lady sings
    Lester's suit wicks moist heat
       her breath   pushes out

       steam bubbles round his collar
   up the hill of his chin   sweat   dances

      he inhales   seals his mouth piece
pours sound down a column

          puffs and streams
    cling to the woolen weave
       of Lady's dress freshen her gardenia

Rice Lady sings   Lester plays *red beans*
    gin   for Lady *wine* for Pres

      these moments   they sing
sweet water rises from their roots.

Behind the Beat

I want that door to open, an old piano
to sound a tune that swings at a walk-about
beat, that tells me to find a pair of spats,
carry a cane or swagger stick, tip my hat,
and go my way with a wink and finger snap.

I see Earl Hines at his keyboard playing
and humming Duke Ellington's "The Shepherd,"
the Duke tap-rap-tapping with his feet,
Earl keeping time with his head,
and me gone looking for my shoes.

These days I take Earl on afternoon walks
to Esser's Pond, swapping song
fragments with ducks and blackbirds,
swallow wings, trills from crickets' legs,
wind stroking cattails and canary grass.

I want Earl next to me when I tramp
in new snow through a city park,
the first tracks before kids and sleds,
moving at a rendezvous pace to meet
some she of my imagination, a ghost

the crisp crunch of boots in fresh snow
calls up, past the lagoon toward the lake,
wind slaps and branches clap, ghosts
double shuffle, slide step, and stamp
like dancers reaching for partners' hands.

I first saw Earl in my college days
making his comeback, playing his brand
of line like solo trumpet, walking bass,
trills that fit with a strolling beat,
and the Duke, the Duke tells a crowd

that *cool* means snapping one's fingers
just   behind   the beat, the way Earl likes it,
while the melody runs upstairs and down,
stops and goes like show-time traffic.
I nod my head, finger-snap, and step out.

I want to walk around like I know something,
listen to musicians chew on notes, leave a set
of footprints in a snowy park, put on some shiny
shoes and learn a little dance, or pretend to,
and don't back off, quit, or discard

until Uncle Death walks down my street
smoking a thin cigar, snapping his fingers
behind   the beat, acting cool while collecting
debts at his leisure, a tap on the shoulder,
a walking bass, keeping time, stepping out.

Shepherd's Return

Imagine Hamelin Town after the pied piper
hypnotized its children into following him
along the winding road into the mountains,
skipping, whistling, singing into disappearance,
all but Willie, the lame boy on crutches, crying and crying,
the aftershock, accusations shouted at the council,
the desperate search parties, dead-end leads,
stored in an archive of dingy cold-case files,
that bleating numbness of daily life that reminds
me of cities in the Ohio of my youth, once smoky
and busy, splendid in their parks and well-lit
streets where plants and mines and warehouses
and shops closed one by one, where the remnant
population lingers on bar stools and the steps
of sagging porches, their children making tracks
for a ride to the future. They're not coming back.

But as one legend begets another, a swig
of musicians slips into town, sent by someone
they call "the Shepherd," to find a hall,
a dialect of faces speaking in a dance of accents
with names like Cat and Cootie and Johnny
who play a syncopated brand of twelve-bar
repeats and dissonant choruses, their rhythm
like bare knuckles beating on an old oak table.
They are the taste of dark ale, a shot of holiday
whiskey, and here comes the Shepherd, Willie,
lame boy from long ago who was too slow to catch
the hilarity of sashaying children before the cave
door in the mountain closed, *the Shepherd*, comes
like a phantom to a used-up Ohio town, his face
a road map of constant travel, his tunic, scarf
and trousers frayed and patched, and saturated

with a satisfaction of dust, balanced and swaying on his good leg, his fingers tapping time, rap-tap-slapping rhythm on the curvature of his crook.

Acknowledgments

Jukebox Junction USA: "The Burning" and "That Mood Indigo."

Reprinted from *Bringer of Songs:* "Two Conversations and a Song."

Tendrils and Tentacles: "The Powers of Singing."

Motif: "Dancing."

Wisconsin Poets' Calendar: "Autumn Whispers" and "This Spring I Will Dream of Mary Lou Williams on Jazz Piano."

Rosebud: "Dance Lessons."

Free Verse: "Tango Lessons."

Verse Wisconsin: "A Tale of One Urban Night"

Wisconsin People & Ideas: "Snow Dance" and "Yes, She's a Jazz Singer."

Wisconsin Trails: "Autumn Scenes for Jazz Combo."

Hummingbird: Magazine of the Short Poem: "Autumn Piece for Jazz Combo."

Yahara Journal: "Jazz at Night, Union Terrace, Madison."

WFOP Museletter: "The '41 Limited."

With thanks to:

Wednesday Afternoon Manuscript Group: Lenore Coberly, Margaret Benbow, Karen Updike, Alice D'Alessio, Robin Chapman, Jeri McCormick, Lynn Patrick Smith, and CX Dillhunt.

Second Monday Manuscript Group: Richard Merelman, Charles Cantrell, Mark Kraushaar, Mark Kliewer, and Rusty Russell.

Bruce Dethlefsen's Poet Camp

Wisconsin Fellowship of Poets

Teachers/Instructors:
Vocal: Christine Seitz and Maggie Delaney-Potthoff.

Tango: Krista Spiro, John Curran, Craig Rypstat, Joe Yang (Wisconsin Tango), Humberto Decima, and dozens of dancers.

Jazz: Joe Luisi, Gypsy Swing Fest, WORT, Isthmus Jazz Fest, and Dave Scheler.

Poetry: Tom McKeown, Alison Townsend, Ellen Kort, Marilyn Taylor, and F. J. Bergmann.

Thanks to my editors: Jeri McCormick, Robin Chapman, CX Dillhunt, and Lynn Patrick and Janet Smith.

Notes

Song:

"Song Full of Flowers," inspired by "You're My Thrill," superb vocal by Helen Merrill on a 6-CD Smithsonian Set.

"Two Conversations and a Song" is based on *Der Tod, das ist die kühle Nacht* (Brahms, German poet) from a brooding, powerful live performance by Christa Ludwig and Leonard Bernstein at Carnegie Hall.

Tango:

Tango is myth legend, glamorous and amorous—all or none of those things. With my paltry Spanish and no trips to Buenos Aires, I became a competent dancer and a good deejay for other dancers—constantly looking for translations.

"A Tale of One Urban Night" is based on a warehouse scene in Sally Potter's film *The Tango Lesson* and driven by Astor Piazzolla's "Libertango," my preferred version, by Gary Burton and Piazzolla's musicians.

"Snow Dance"—I use "Á Los Amigos," because the melody is right.

"Late-Night Thoughts on the Tango"—Bob Barres' class "Tempranillo."

"The Day After" inspired by "El Día Después" by Carlos Libedinsky from the CD *Narcotango 2*—brooding metaphors.

Jazz:

"Behind the Beat" and "Shepherd's Return" used Earl Hines' piano rendition of Duke Ellington's "The Shepherd" (Second Sacred Concert) from a superb 2-CD set of Duke Ellington's music by Earl Hines.

About the Author

Ohio-born, New Jersey-bred, Wisconsin-gleaned Richard Roe beat, tapped and danced his way through his musical repertoire whenever it pleased him. "Sins of my old age," he often said. Richard was an influential part of the Wisconsin poetry scene for over forty years. His schedule was filled with poetry readings—as a reader, audience member, and organizer. He published three books of poetry: *What Will You Find at the Edge of the World?* and *Bringer of Songs*, both from Fireweed Press, and *Knots of Sweet Longing* from Wolfsong Publications. His work has appeared in numerous publications including *Wisconsin People & Ideas, Verse Wisconsin, Free Verse, Stoneboat, Writing by Ear: An Anthology of Writing About Music, Come What May: An Anthology of Writings about Chance, Jukebox Junction USA,* and *River Poems.* Historian, economist, Legislative Analyst, but always a singer. RIP, 1941–2019.